This book belongs to:

_____

Lisa	
Yolanda	plates
Jolene	forks
Cat	cups
Denise	napkins
Chelsea	wine glasses
Debbie	

chic fil a	chips/dip
mac n cheese	dessert
beef sliders	
pizza	soda
hot dogs	wine
	water
	cocktails

wine tasting
   wine glasses
   Kit

Clean powder room

Stairway

Family room

Kitchen